Original title:
Garden Gazes

Copyright © 2025 Creative Arts Management OÜ
All rights reserved.

Author: Seraphina Caldwell
ISBN HARDBACK: 978-1-80566-696-7
ISBN PAPERBACK: 978-1-80566-981-4

Secrets Beneath the Roots

Worms exchange whispers deep in the soil,
As butterflies gossip while basking in toil.
Rabbits debate which patch is the best,
While the snails move slowly, never in jest.

A dandelion dreams of being a queen,
Flaunting bright petals, all fluffy and green.
Ants march like soldiers, in columns they go,
While ladybugs giggle, stealing the show.

Enchantment in Every Bloom

Roses wear crowns, thorns all a-glow,
Tulips play patty-cake, putting on a show.
Sunflowers twist, just to catch a glance,
While violets take part in a dainty dance.

The daisies have secrets they whisper at night,
Wishing for moonbeams to make them feel light.
Peonies puff out, trying to look grand,
While marigolds chuckle, by sun's warm hand.

The Canvas of Time's Gentle Hand

Poppies paint pictures of summers gone by,
As bees don aprons, preparing to fly.
The lilies hold hands, so prim and so neat,
While mint tells tales of the best things to eat.

Bramble berries argue, sweet but so sly,
With each little squabble, they nibble and pry.
While shadows do jiggles, beneath leafy art,
All while the breeze plays the craziest part.

Serenity Under Blossoming Canopies

Under the branches where shadows play,
The squirrels hold conferences daily at bay.
The chipmunks play poker, all chips made of seeds,
While robins sing songs to fulfill all their needs.

The cherries are blushing with sweet little grins,
As frogs play leapfrog, practicing spins.
With laughter and whispers, the critters confide,
In the shade of the treetops, joy's opened wide.

The Breath of Wild Meadows

In fields so wild and bright,
A squirrel stole my sandwich bite.
I chased him down with a loud shout,
He laughed, then dashed—my lunch thrown out.

A butterfly waved goodbye,
While bees buzzed in a rush to fly.
They think they own this sunny space,
I just wanted a little grace.

The daisies danced all day long,
While a rabbit hopped to a tune, a song.
But when I tried to join the fun,
They giggled hard and said, 'You run!'

Twilight's Caress on Colorful Leaves

As day turns dim, the colors swirl,
A beetle's on a mad dance furl.
He twirls and spins on leafy green,
While I just trip, looking quite mean.

The sunset waves a brush of gold,
While crickets chirp tales of old.
A grasshopper in pensive pose,
Yells, 'Dare you to jump!'—Oh, how it goes!

Shadows stretch, and laughter grows,
With fireflies playing peek-a-boos.
I'm caught in nature's silly spell,
As dusk and dawn bid their farewell.

Children of the Sun and Soil

Little ants march like a parade,
With tiny flags that never fade.
They bump and tumble, lose their way,
I chuckle, thinking they need a stay.

A ladybug, a dot of cheer,
Sipped dew drops from a flower near.
But when it slipped, what a scene!
It tumbled down—quite the routine!

Earthworms wriggle, making a fuss,
Saying, 'We'll use your shoe for a bus!'
They giggle as they squirm and wiggle,
While I just stand, trying not to giggle.

Nature's Silent Conversations

Two trees gossip in the breeze,
While a rabbit tries to squeeze.
He nibbles grass, while they complain,
Of squirrels, acorns, and the rain.

A cloud drifts by with a dreamy sigh,
Casting shadows where daisies lie.
They whisper secrets to the night,
About the moon, so bold and bright.

Frogs croak jokes, a tadpole's grin,
As crickets strum their nightly din.
In nature's lore, they always sing,
Of simple things and all they bring.

A Tapestry Woven with Petal Threads

A bee in a bow tie, quite the sight,
Buzzing to the flowers, oh what delight!
Daisies wear hats, all puffed and proud,
While tulips gossip, among the crowd.

Ladybugs dance, in peppy shoes,
While daisies debate the latest news.
A snail in shades gives a slow-roast joke,
As mushrooms chuckle, in earthy cloak.

Dawn's Kiss on Flowering Dreams

Morning yawns, with sleepy eyes,
As sunbeams tickle, no surprise.
The roses giggle, with dew on their cheeks,
While sunflowers swoon, like stars in their peaks.

The daisies break into a morning cheer,
As squirrels chase shadows, devoid of fear.
A butterfly winks, in colors so bright,
While the rest of the blooms say, 'What a sight!'

The Enigma of Nature's Beauty

A purple petal mystifies the lawn,
Declaring itself the chosen one's dawn.
With a mustache made of clover so neat,
It claims all the soil beneath its feet.

The grass chuckles softly, sly and spry,
As a worm in a top hat gives it a try.
Ferns throw a party, with fronds in the air,
While ants take a break from their wild affair.

Flourishing Spirits in Quiet Corners

In shadowy nooks, the daisies sneak,
Plotting their mischief, wearily unique.
A chubby little hedgehog snorts in delight,
As dandelions giggle, taking flight.

While bunnies discuss a rare carrot heist,
With stories so wild, they'd make you crack!
A toad croaks jokes in a sludgy cap,
As the evening light starts to unwrap.

Conversations in Flora's Language

The daisies gossip in the breeze,
While buttercups dance with such ease.
Tulips roll their eyes with flair,
"Did you see that bee? What a hair!"

Lavender starts a rumor or two,
"I heard the roses are feeling blue!"
While sunflowers laugh in a tall parade,
"We're all just waiting for the next charade!"

The Spirit of All Things Growing

A sprout said, "I've got my groove,"
"Just wait till I really move!"
The carrots joke about their height,
"It's tough being orange, but feels just right!"

The tomatoes turn red with glee,
"Why are we blushing? Wait and see!"
Cucumbers giggle, oh so green,
"Pecked by birds, we're their food scene!"

Beyond the Whispering Boughs

The oak tree chuckled, "Keep it down!"
"Can't hear the squirrels, they're such clowns!"
Maples swayed, whispering sly,
"Why does the wind never say goodbye?"

Pine cones dropped with playful grace,
"Is it just me, or can you feel space?"
Birds perched high in cheeky rows,
"They think they own us! Ha, who knows?"

The Veil of Satin Petals

Roses wore their finest dress,
"Are you going out? You look a mess!"
Violets chimed in, a quirky crew,
"We'll hold a party—just for two!"

The lilies giggled, white and grand,
"Let's all start a flower band!"
Poppies swayed to the silly tune,
"We'll dance until we see the moon!"

Shadows Play Among the Blooms

In a patch of sun, a bee did dance,
He tripped on petals, missed his chance.
A ladybug laughed; oh what a sight,
As butterflies giggled, taking flight.

A dandelion puffed, feeling so grand,
But then a gust came, oh, wasn't it planned?
Seeds flew like confetti all over the ground,
While flowers just chuckled, their heads spinning 'round.

Hues of Hope in Every Stem

A tulip wore shoes that were far too tight,
Wiggled and jiggled, oh what a plight!
"Why must I wear these?" cried out in despair,
While daisies just giggled without a care.

The marigolds rolled in colors so bright,
As violets whispered, "This feels just right!"
Each bloom had a story, each hue had a tale,
In every petal's laughter, we find a holy grail.

The Language of Nature's Heart

Roses debated who's best in the crowd,
They boasted and blushed, getting quite loud.
But thorns interjected with a sharp little jest,
"Without us," they said, "you'd be less than the best!"

A sunflower winked and turned to the sun,
"Let's all be silly, let's just have some fun!"
The leaves swayed and giggled, the roots held a cheer,
In the chatter of nature, we find delight here.

Petals and Memories Entwined

The wind told a tale of a cluster of blooms,
Who once threw a party, all dressed in costumes.
With petals for hats and stems tied with bows,
They danced in the breeze, struck a funny pose.

An old oak tree sighed, "What a curious scene,
Wouldn't it be grand if we all were just green?"
But laughter erupted from every color there,
In petals and memories, joy fills the air.

The Allure of a Secret Path

In the bushes, a squirrel prances,
Chasing shadows and lost chances.
A rabbit hops, with a wobbly dance,
Who knew he had such fancy pants?

The hidden trail beckons with glee,
But is that a flower or a bumblebee?
One step forward, a leap of faith,
Oh dear, did I just lose my brace?

Where Nature's Paintbrush Strokes

A butterfly flaunts its colorful attire,
While the ants march like a tiny choir.
They're painting the blooms in wild disarray,
Who knew nature had its own cabaret?

With colors splashed in laughter's hue,
Petals sway as if they just flew.
Each bloom, a portrait, a jest, a thrill,
Dancing to rhythms of the gentle hill.

Moments of Serenity in Green

A lizard sunbathes with utmost pride,
While bees buzz near, a joyride tide.
The grass tickles toes with a gentle tease,
Just don't ask the mole to say cheese!

The trees hold secrets, whisper low,
From acorns who dream of being a show.
I sat to ponder on life's little quirks,
And a crow chimed in with its odd smirks.

Whirlwind of Scented Reverie

Fragrant flowers throw a wild bash,
While the daisies throw caution to the crash.
The roses giggle, oh what a sight,
As the lavender winks in the waning light.

The wind brings tales, both funny and bold,
Of petunias that gossip and sunflowers that scold.
In this scented delight, all senses engage,
Who knew nature's whimsy took center stage?

Beneath the Canopy of Dreams

Underneath the leafy hats,
The squirrels dance like acrobats.
With every twist, a playful spin,
They giggle loud, let the fun begin.

A ladybug with polka spots,
Teases ants in funny knots.
They march in tune, their tiny feet,
A circus act that can't be beat.

A flower sways with gentle grace,
Winking at bees with a silly face.
The pollen floats like tiny gold,
A treasure hunt for young and old.

The breeze pulls pranks upon the trees,
Whispers secrets with playful ease.
In this realm where laughter blooms,
Joy erupts, as nature blooms.

The Soul of the Wildflower

A wildflower sings, off-key yet proud,
Who knew it could shout so loud?
Beneath the sun, it waves hello,
In a patch where goofy things grow.

The bees all buzz in frantic haste,
Dancing round in honeyed haste.
They hold a waltz, with feet on loan,
In the heart of nature's funny zone.

A dandelion puffs its chest,
Challenging clouds, it's simply the best.
With laughter bright, it scatters its seeds,
Like wishes made for whimsical deeds.

In this place where blooms take flight,
Life's a circus, what a delight!
Each petal whispers, each stem debates,
Nature's humor, it celebrates!

Shadows of the Sunlit Grove

In the grove where shadows play,
Frogs tell jokes about the day.
They leap on logs, with tiny cheer,
Croaking out what all would hear.

The sunbeams tickle tips of leaves,
Creating shadows that dance and tease.
Every flicker brings giggles near,
As the woodpecker drums a funny cheer.

A rabbit hops with flair and style,
With floppy ears that make you smile.
He nibbles clovers, oh so neat,
Wearing grass like a fashionable sheet.

Laughter echoes through the scene,
In this grove, fun reigns supreme.
Every rustle, a tale to be told;
In nature's arms, the heart is bold.

Lullabies of the Hidden Glen

In the glen where moonlight beams,
Crickets play their silly themes.
A chorus sings, with a twisty tune,
To soothe the night beneath the moon.

Fireflies blink like tiny stars,
Forming patterns of giggles and bars.
Dance a jig, they twinkle bright,
Filling the darkness with joyful light.

The owls wink in their feathered suits,
Making puns from tree to roots.
With every hoot, a nudge, a poke,
Their midnight humor, a gentle joke.

Napkins made from leaves and dew,
Nature's picnic for me and you.
In this glen, laughter is found,
As dreams take flight, all around.

Whispers of Petal Dreams

The tulips talk in hushed tones,
A gossip fest on flowered phones.
Daisies giggle, gossip in stir,
While roses blush, oh what a blur.

Bee's buzz a joke, it's hard to hear,
They tickle blooms, then disappear.
Petals dance, they make a scene,
Sharing tales that might have been.

Buds hold secrets, whispered so light,
While marigolds grumble, they're just too bright.
Sunflowers grin, they won't be late,
Swapping tales about their fate.

In this patch, laughter blooms wide,
With every breeze, petals collide.
Nature's jests in colors parade,
A wild frolic, never to fade.

Sunlight's Gentle Caress

Sunlight sneezes, oh what a sight,
The shadows scatter, laugh in delight.
A daffodil yawns, stretches its stem,
Claiming it's always the best in the den.

Ladybugs twirl, on leaf they hop,
Chasing their tails, never a stop.
The sun winks, demanding a game,
While all of the blooms play, who gets the fame?

Pumpkins giggle, they wear silly grins,
Wagering who'll roll in sunny spins.
Butterflies flaunt their outfits so grand,
As dandelions scatter, wanting more land.

With each drop of light, the fun expands,
In this bright space where nature stands.
Buds bloom with laughter, colors bold,
As sunlight's touch turns warm from cold.

The Secret Life of Blossoms

In the moonlight, flowers confide,
The secrets they hold, nowhere to hide.
The lilies gossip, with smiles so sly,
"Did you hear what the petunias imply?"

Cacti chuckle, they're prickly and proud,
Yet share their stories, speaking out loud.
Peonies boast, they're the stars of the show,
Making a scene wherever they grow.

Wind whispers tales of celestial cheer,
As budding blooms spread giggles far and near.
Orchids roll eyes, "So last year's trend,"
Watching as nature's rivalries bend.

Each color a punchline in life's bright act,
With petals exchanging the silliest fact.
In this realm of lush hues and sound,
Beneath quiet leaves, laughter is found.

In Bloom's Embrace

Daisies unite for a silly debate,
Who's the prettiest, it just won't wait.
Marigolds boast with vibrant delight,
While violets quip, "Hey, 'size' is a fright!"

Bees gather round, buzzing their cheer,
With a pitter-patter that's hard to hear.
Flowers frown when a breeze blows through,
Whispering truths they never thought true.

Snapdragons grin, all in good jest,
Trading their tales, who's faring the best.
A wallflower blushes, says "I'm just shy,"
Yet all of the blooms give a wink and a sigh.

In this playful patch of laughter and light,
Nature's mischief unfolds every night.
With petals entwined in a whimsical dance,
Life in full bloom gives the heart a chance.

In the Embrace of Earth's Palette

Bees wear tiny hats, you see,
Buzzing as they sip their tea.
Roses giggle, thorns in sight,
A prickly party, what a sight!

Daffodils dance, with bows so bright,
They twirl and swirl, a pure delight.
Tulips gossip, petals aflame,
Who knew flowers could be so lame?

Worms host a game of hide and seek,
In the soil, they take a peek.
While snails race with shells so grand,
Winning slowly, just as planned!

Under the sun, laughter flows,
Nature's antics, who really knows?
In this patch, joy's on display,
A whimsical world where flowers play.

Children of the Flora

Butterflies wearing silly shoes,
Fluttering about, sharing the news.
Ladybugs play hopscotch on leaves,
Counting spots as the sun weaves.

The daisies whisper silly jokes,
While tulips chuckle, no need for blokes.
In this realm where whimsy bloats,
A frog croaks songs in amusing notes.

With bees as DJs, buzzing tunes,
Pollen parties under bright moons.
Frolicsome ferns wave from their beds,
Encouraging fun with leafy threads.

In this wild, floral playground dream,
Life is a laugh, or so it seems.
Nature's jesters, in colors they gleam,
Making merriment the leading theme.

Palette of the Heart's Eden

Sunflowers strut in tall bands,
Waving like they've got fans.
Petunias wear shades, oh so cool,
Growing charisma, they rule the school!

The cabbage shakes its leafy pom-poms,
While carrots recite silly taunts and psalms.
Beetles host debates in the shade,
Polling the flowers on whom to invade.

Rabbits hop by with mischief in tow,
Testing the waters, here to bestow.
With sneaky grins, they plot and prance,
In the realm of blooms, it's a crazy dance!

Every petal shares a witty tale,
Through laughter and joy, they set sail.
In this Eden where colors collide,
A funny fest, where mirth's our guide.

Hues of Dawn on Leafy Canvases

Morning dew drops like jewels fair,
While flowers stretch without a care.
Sunrise paints with a joyful hand,
Oil pastels in this wacky land.

Butterflies brush up on their skills,
Practicing pirouettes, for the thrills.
Daisies giggle beneath the sky,
Giving each other a cheery nigh!

With petals ooh-ing as colors bloom,
Even the weeds get caught in the room.
A daffodil on a soapbox stands,
Telling jokes while the garden bands.

Laughter echoes through the trees,
As mother nature sprinkles breeze.
In this canvas where hues unite,
Funny moments shine oh so bright.

Melodies of Growth and Renewal

In the sun, the daisies dance,
Winking at the bees in trance.
A squirrel steals a juicy pear,
While a bunny hops without a care.

Worms compose a bassoon band,
As flowers giggle, close at hand.
With every sprout, mischief brews,
Nature's jesters in bright hues.

The snapdragons plot a play,
With daisies leading on the way.
Laughter blooms on every vine,
As shrubs wear hats, oh so fine!

Among the weeds a party grows,
Orchids gossip, nobody knows.
In this realm of light and cheer,
Funny friends are always near.

An Ode to the Whispering Blooms

Tulips tattle on the breeze,
Dandelions shout, "Take it, please!"
Bees buzz like a tipsy choir,
While tulips reveal their secret fire.

The violets tease the daffodils,
Who sway like they've got popping thrills.
As petals chuckle in delight,
One sunflower begins a fright!

The roses roll their eyes in jest,
And proclaim, "We're simply the best!"
Snapdragons shoot their witty quips,
While untamed vines sprout funny flips.

Petunias plot a flower show,
In hopes their humor starts to grow.
In this colorful, silly space,
Every bloom wears a cheerful face!

Whispers Among Petals

In a patch of vibrant cheer,
All the flowers gather near.
Lilies giggle, shade their eyes,
As wind whispers rude goodbyes.

The tulips boast of perfect style,
While weeds just lounge, sans a trial.
"A flower with no petals, please,"
Claims the grass, tickling knees.

With each day, the pollen jests,
As butterflies wear daisy vests.
"Polinate, my friends!" they sing,
While crickets join and start to swing.

In this plot of love and glee,
Every bloom holds a key.
They laugh and bloom and stretch their might,
Turning mundane days to pure delight.

Echoes of a Blooming Dawn

At dawn, the petals start to cheer,
The grasshoppers dance without a fear.
A flamboyant cactus shares a joke,
While morning mist begins to choke.

The daffodils joke with the breeze,
"Can you hear the ants' loud sneeze?"
Sloppy dew drips, what a sight,
As ladybugs perform in flight.

Marigolds laugh in silent glee,
"Why did the bee fly up a tree?"
"Who knows!" shout the daisies, "Let's ask!
Then watch the sun rise as our task."

With every bloom, giggles rise,
What a fun surprise in the skies!
In this patch where mischief sprouts,
We find joy, amidst the shouts.

Echoing Laughter of Sprouting Life

Rabbits hop with goofy grace,
Chasing shadows, joining the race.
Sunflowers peek with big, bright grins,
While ants hold tiny violin skins.

Worms wiggle in a snazzy dance,
While daisies twirl in a playful trance.
Bumbling bees with their fuzzy hats,
Buzz around in silly spats.

Frogs leap high, they go quite far,
Kicking up mud like a wild car.
While ladybugs sip on dewdrop tea,
Sipping slowly, oh what glee!

And in this frolic, laughter's heard,
Among the leaves, without a word.
A symphony of gleeful sights,
As life blooms under sunny lights.

Nature's Lens on Forgotten Paths

A squirrel poses on a rocking branch,
Flexing paws while he takes a chance.
The wind whispers snickers through the trees,
As all the leaves giggle in the breeze.

Caterpillars wear jackets far too large,
While beetles play cards, they take charge.
With acorns stacked in a wobbly heap,
They laugh it up, not losing sleep.

A snail slides by with a slow, grand bow,
While flowers cheer, 'Take a bow now!'
And frogs croak jokes with quite a flair,
As bubbles rise and dance in air.

Each step reveals the playful jest,
In paths that nature loves the best.
So follow along with a chuckle and grin,
Where laughter and whimsy always win.

Beauty in the Every Leaf

Leaves wear colors like fancy dress,
Whirling in wind, they make a mess.
The little ones cheer, 'Look at us spin!'
While acorns conspire in a cheeky din.

Each tiny bud has a story to tell,
Of insects that giggle and pollen that fell.
With chirping birds providing the song,
Nature's comedy never goes wrong.

A worm trails by with a grin so sly,
Singing to flowers, 'Hey, watch me fly!'
Blades of grass whisper silly secrets,
While crickets compete for the best of the crests.

In every leaf, a smile we find,
As laughter spreads to every kind.
Here's hoping your heart joins in the fun,
Where nature's humor shines like the sun.

Petal Poetry of the Wind

Petals dance like a lively crew,
Spinning stories only they knew.
Dandelions giggle, take to the sky,
As clouds roll in with a soft, fluff sigh.

Bees recite verses full of delight,
While draping sunlight in golden light.
Flowers grin wide, their petals in bloom,
As a gentle breeze swoops through the room.

A poppy tells tales, and daisies respond,
With whimsical lines that they fondly bond.
The violets hum, their voices do twine,
Creating a chorus that's simply divine.

So listen close to nature's sweet cheer,
In every petal, laughter draws near.
For in this vast dance of color and sound,
The joy of existence is always found.

Seeds of Wonder in Nature's Eyes

In patchy rows, they whisper loud,
Small sproutlings peek from the soft shroud.
A turnip dreams of Broadway fame,
While radishes play a rooty game.

Under sun's dance, they sip and twirl,
Dandelions blow, what a swirl!
"I'm the king!" a crow boasts near,
While worms in tuxes take their cheer.

A carrot shakes, its leafy crown,
"Who needs a bath in this brown town?"
Cucumbers gossip 'neath broad leaves,
Laughing at all the prankster thieves.

Each seedling giggles, a sprouts' delight,
In soil's embrace, they share the night.
With every breeze, they nod and sway,
Chasing bugs that come out to play.

Serenade of the Seasonal Rhythms

Spring hops in with a bright bouquet,
While winter grumbles, "Not today!"
A sneezy bloom lets out a cheer,
"Catch me on blooms' best of year!"

Summer flips pancakes in the sun,
While spinach swims, it's all in fun.
"Is it hot?" calls out the sweet pea,
"Grab some lemonade; come sit with me!"

Autumn strums on a leafy lute,
Pumpkins ready for a brand new suit.
"Who left the door ajar?" asks thyme,
"Don't let the frost sneak in this time!"

Each season shimmies, struts in line,
Nature's rhythm—a funny sign.
With every mix-up and bump, they play,
In the dance of life, they frolic away.

Sowing the Seeds of Forgotten Dreams

Once I planted a dream of a pie,
But the berries laughed and bid goodbye.
"Not today, we're off to the fair!"
So I watered my thoughts with a prayer.

A rose told tales of grandeur lost,
Where tulips sneaked in and bravely tossed.
"I'll be famous!" said a green bean sprout,
While carrots cheered, "What's it all about?"

A worm spun tales of wishes old,
"Hurry! Hurry! We've dreams untold!"
While peas make puns about their plight,
"Each pod a joke, oh what a sight!"

So here I stand with a watering can,
Pouring hopes like a cheerful fan.
With laughter sprouting from every seam,
In a world where we sow our dreams.

Nature's Breath Between the Blooms

Breezes whisper jokes to the bees,
As daisies snicker with utmost ease.
"Could a sunflower reach the stars?"
"No way, buddy, you'll just make cars!"

The tulips waltz in a floral ball,
While pesky bugs plot to make a call.
"Who's the brightest?" asks a shy moss,
"To win my heart, you'll have to toss!"

A breeze tickles leaves, laughter's spread,
"Come on, grass, let's raise a thread!"
Dandelions dream of flying high,
As butterflies wink and wave bye-bye.

In this patch, life's a funny game,
Where blooms debate who's to blame.
So take a breath—between the gales,
Join the chuckle, where each one prevails.

The Dance of the Sunlit Ferns

A fern in the sun starts to twirl,
It rustles and giggles like a little girl.
With leaves in the breeze, they jig and they sway,
Inviting the bugs to come dance and play.

A ladybug slides down a tall stalk,
Telling the ants it's a perfect talk.
They laugh at the beetle who thinks he's so grand,
While crickets chirp in this leafy band.

Sunbeams peek through, casting shadows that chase,
As petals get tangled in a frolicsome race.
The grass stretches out, tickling toes all around,
In this silly ballet on the soft, mossy ground.

With laughter so bright, chirps fill the air,
Nature's own dance, a whimsical affair.
So come join the fun in this leafy parade,
Where each playful glance is a masterpiece made.

Tapestry of Earthly Joys

Under petals so colorful, a snail makes his way,
Claiming he's racing, though it's a slow play.
He mutters to flowers, 'Just look at my speed!'
While bees buzz by, with a comic stampede.

A hedgehog rolls in a ball full of pride,
Making the bunnies all laugh, though they hide.
'Look at my spikes, aren't they just the best?'
While thistles around him just humor the jest.

The sunflowers lean in to whisper and chat,
About the clumsy birds who land with a splat.
Their graceful ballet of flaps and flops,
Is the hit of the day, with giggles that drop.

In every bright corner, such joy does unfold,
With butterflies flaunting their colors so bold.
The tapestry woven with laughter and cheer,
Is stitched with a smile that we all hold dear.

Beneath the Lattice of Time

Where shadows play tricks between branches and leaves,
A raccoon complains, 'These are not my best eves!'
With a twinkle of mischief under moonlight's gleam,
He eyes all the snacks like it's part of a dream.

The owls hoot laughter, yes, wise with a grin,
As the raccoon tumbles, trying to spin.
'You'll never catch me, I'm clever and quick!'
But the laughing crickets just call him a trick.

Each twinkling star winks down at the fuss,
As fireflies gather, their glow makes a plus.
They dance in time, with laughter that chimes,
Creating a riddle in whimsical rhymes.

As night winds down, and the antics do fade,
The raccoon replays all the fun he has made.
With a bow to the moon, so bright up above,
He curls up in dreams full of nature and love.

A Sojourn Through Sunlit Canopies

With a skip and a hop, the squirrels explore,
Chasing each other, they leap and they score.
Whirling in circles, they seem to tease,
While teasing the shadows that sway in the breeze.

The mushrooms are giggling, it's hard to believe,
As fungi unite with tales up their sleeve.
One says it's magic, the other, a wish,
As they dance on the ground, seeking the swish.

Above, the birds sing their sweetest refrain,
Yet down on the floor, there's a knitting campaign.
A rabbit, a badger, and quite a few folks,
Sewing flower crowns, sharing jokes and pokes.

In this lively retreat where the brows furrow free,
Each critter invites you to hop and be glee.
So let's laugh together with joy all around,
In this sunny escape where silliness is found.

The Art of Stillness in Nature

In the stillness, beetles stare,
Pondering life on a leaf with flair.
Bumblebees hum a hasty tune,
While ants hold meetings under the moon.

A snail in slow motion breaks the speed,
Wearing its shell, hoping to succeed.
A bird drops a twig with a sneeze,
Thinking it's art — oh please, oh please!

A breeze whispers secrets, quite absurd,
Tickling the petals, it's such a word.
Flowers giggle with colors so bright,
As butterflies dance, taking flight.

So ponder the art of doing very little,
In nature's realm, don't settle or whittle.
Every critter around has a role to play,
In the comical chaos of nature's ballet.

Chronicles of Morning Dew

Morning dew drips like a clumsy gem,
Jewels on petals, oh, what a whim!
A moth sneezes, causing a stir,
Landing nearby with a soft little blur.

Grass tickles toes, in sunlight it glows,
While spiders spin webs in elaborate throes.
A beetle rolls leaves like a great big ball,
Thinking it's fit for a grand insect hall.

The sun peeks through, a curious fellow,
Highlights the dew's pearly yellow.
As drips fall down in a startled race,
A squirrel looks up with a puzzled face.

Chasing the light, all creatures engage,
In morning's tales, how they set the stage.
Each droplet a story, no need for a cue,
In the chronicles draped in morning dew.

Reflections in Floral Mirrors

In floral mirrors, the world gets distorted,
Petals reflect what can't be reported.
A bee admires its golden attire,
In daisies' frames, it thinks it's a sire.

A ladybug wore a polka-dot dream,
While pondering life, or so it would seem.
With nearby blossoms giggling in time,
Every bloom bursting with color and rhyme.

The butterflies preen like they own the show,
Whispering secrets that only they know.
As they strike a pose in the perfect light,
Rabbits look on, eyes wide with delight.

In reflections of color, pure and bright,
Nature's own canvas brings laughter and light.
Though silliness reigns in this floral parade,
Every glance echoes joy that won't fade.

Serenade of the Wildflowers

In fields of colors, wildflowers sway,
Sipping on sunshine, they frolic and play.
The daisies debate who's the prettiest scene,
While dandelions giggle, causing a scene.

A butterfly slips, but oh what a grace,
Landing on petals, a whimsical place.
Bees buzz about with a coffee shop's mood,
Chasing each other, it's quite the brood!

A frog joins the choir, croaks loud like a bard,
Claiming the spotlight, oh, isn't it hard?
The sun sets low, with a pink cotton candy,
Nature's own concert, both silly and dandy.

With crickets ensemble, a rhythmic surprise,
Stars peek in, with twinkling eyes.
In the serenade sung all through the night,
Wildflowers laugh, till morning's first light.

Tapestry of Nature's Eye

In the patch where daisies talk,
A bee forgot his route to walk.
He buzzed a tune, oh what a sight,
While daisies laughed at his delight.

A worm in shades of rainbow bright,
Took offense, and gave a bite.
The plants all shook, like they were scared,
'That worm's fashion? How is it aired?'

The sun came up, with beams on show,
And butterflies danced to and fro.
A party here, with veggies dressed,
In leafy suits, they all impressed.

The squash tried to juggle in vain,
While pumpkins rolled, like boats in rain.
The air was thick with laughter's sound,
In this wild patch, pure joy was found.

Reflections in the Garden's Heart

A gnome in red with a crooked grin,
Chased after squirrels with a spin.
He stumbled here, he tumbled there,
The flowers giggled with great flair.

Tomatoes argued which was round,
While spinach frowned, it sighed profound.
'Why must we squabble?' lettuce cried,
'We all should bask in sunshine's pride!'

The herbs exchanged their secret tips,
On charm and style and funny quips.
A mint decided to wear a tie,
While chives all sighed, and asked him why.

The moon peeked in, a curious sight,
To see such chaos, full of light.
With giggles echoing through the night,
In this wild place, all felt just right.

Murmurs in the Meadow

The blades of grass held whispered dreams,
While frogs croaked out their silly themes.
A snail strutted in its shiny shell,
Claiming 'I'm the fastest, can't you tell?'

The butterflies wore fancy hats,
Gossiping 'bout the snooty cats.
They played croquet with daffodils,
While crickets sang of clashing wills.

A dandelion puffed in pride,
'I'm the best, just look inside!'
But when the wind gave it a blow,
It lost its fluff, and said, 'Oh no!'

As daisies danced beneath the sky,
A squirrel tripped, oh my, oh my!
Laughter echoed through the grove,
In this bright world, joy was wove.

A Symphony of Colors

The roses blushed in shades so bright,
While violets donned their evening light.
A sunflower twirled in days gone past,
Declared, 'I'm tall, and that's a blast!'

The marigolds played in a band,
With bumblebees lending a hand.
The peonies puffed with graceful flair,
In this music, there was no care.

A daisy claimed it was the star,
'I'll shine, despite this gossip far!'
The tulips chimed, 'In stripes we shine,
Together we bloom, all things divine!'

Night fell softly, the colors glowed,
This painted world, where laughter flowed.
And in this chaos, one could see,
A tapestry of joy, wild and free.

Twilight's Embrace in Flora's Realm

The daisies dance with glee at night,
While crickets sing their tunes just right.
A sleepy rose drips with surprise,
As fireflies wink with flashing eyes.

The marigold spills secrets, loud,
To passing bees who form a crowd.
Meanwhile, tanglefoot keeps a score,
Of ants who march and bump, encore!

The Forage of Time and Bloom

In the wild, a dandelion's plight,
To float away just feels so right.
While thistles scratch with pointy grace,
A ladybug just won the race!

The sunflowers chuckle as they race,
With necks so long, they take up space.
The butterflies are quite the show,
Critics with wings—they steal the glow!

Buds of Memories

A tulip trips on its own shoe,
While pansies play peekaboo,
Their laughter bursts like fragrant air,
"Oh! Watch your step, with such flair!"

The violets giggle, all a-sway,
Counting how many birds can play.
A petal falls with dramatic flair,
"I'm just too pretty, beware!"

Sunlit Strokes of Nature

The sun paints smiles on all the leaves,
As squirrels play tricks, oh, how it weaves!
A daffodil caught in mid-yawn,
"Who knew bright blooms could look so drawn?"

The butterflies battle for the best,
While bumblebees buzz with zest.
"Hey, don't take that nectar," they scream,
In this funny, flowery dream!

Through the Veil of Blossoms

Amid the blooms, a bumblebee,
Waltzes like it's fancy-free.
Petals wave, they sing and sway,
As gnomes just laugh the day away.

A dogwood tree, with branches wide,
Tries to fit in, but takes a ride.
The sunflowers gossip, tall and proud,
While daisies dance, just a bit loud.

A snail's parade, they move so slow,
With ambitions high, but nowhere to go.
They huddle close, they plot and scheme,
Dreaming big, but with no real dream.

Butterflies wear the latest trends,
They flutter by, making amends.
Every bloom, a clownish face,
In this radiant, silly place.

Canvas of the Spirit's Meadow

A rabbit dons a tiny hat,
Trying to look like a cool cat.
With shades on, he hops, a sight to see,
Bopping along, all wild and free.

Crickets play their evening tunes,
While frogs croak out their funny prunes.
Grass blades giggle, sway in jest,
Mirth fills this space, a lovely fest.

A squirrel glides, a daring feat,
Mistaking branches for the street.
He spins and twists, a nutty dive,
In this wild place, they all survive.

With every leaf a quirky tale,
Whispering secrets, filled with ale.
The wind chuckles, soft and bright,
In this meadow, pure delight.

Scented Journeys Through Twisted Vines

A vine curls up, a cheeky twist,
On a quest for the perfect tryst.
It bumps a fence, and falls right down,
Wishing it could run around town.

Mice hold a meeting, who's to be queen?
Plan in place for a cheese cuisine.
They giggle and run, a stealthy group,
Over grass blades, they low-key stoop.

With every leaf, a story's spun,
Adventures shared, oh what fun!
As shadows stretch, the day's grown old,
The fruit is ripe, the laughter bold.

A ladybug, with spots askew,
Tries to figure out what's new.
With a wiggle and a charming pose,
She claims the crown, where adventure flows.

A Serenade for Leafy Lovers

Two thistles in a love embrace,
Competing now for garden space.
They poke and prod, but giggle loud,
In thistledom, they stand so proud.

A tulip swoops in for the flair,
With petals bright, it steals the air.
"Look at me!" it shouts with glee,
Just wanting love from every bee.

Dandelions whisper, secrets sneak,
With fluff and dreams, their futures peak.
They scatter seeds on zephyr's breath,
Playing a game, defying death.

These leafy hearts, in playful dance,
Find joy in every fleeting chance.
They twirl and whirl, through sun and rain,
In this vibrant, silly terrain.

Where Butterflies Dare to Dance

In a patch of sunlight, bugs do prance,
They twirl and dip, oh what a chance!
A ladybug in a top hat sways,
While ants march on in funny ballet.

Bees tease flowers, buzz with glee,
Daisies whisper secrets, just for me.
A butterfly flaps, takes a bow,
Joining the frolic, oh, and how!

Tulips giggle, a party in bloom,
Petals swirl like a feathered plume.
The sunbeam jests, casting rays of light,
Nature's vaudeville, a comic delight!

In this merry patch, all sing and sway,
Where joy spills out in a bright bouquet.
Oh what a sight, this playful romance,
Where butterflies dare to take a chance!

Echoes of Verdant Tranquility

A snail dressed up in a fancy shell,
Wobbles and slides, oh what a swell!
While frogs hold court on lily pads,
Croaking their jokes, making me glad.

The trees are gossiping, rustling leaves,
Telling tales of mischief, oh, good grief!
Squirrels swing by on a minty spree,
Nuts in their cheeks, wild and free.

A dandy dandelion winks at me,
Says, 'Life's too short, come laugh with me!'
The sun starts winking, day turns to night,
In this hug of nature, all feels right.

Whispers of the wild, in breezy cheer,
Where each chuckle is sweet and near.
In this serene space, hearts are set free,
An echo of joys, that's the key!

A Symphony of Vibrant Colors

In a riot of hues, the flowers fight,
Roses in red, a dazzling sight!
A sunflower winks, 'I'm the star here!'
While violets pout, 'That's just sheer!'

The poppies giggle in their bright attire,
Swirling and whirling, oh, such a choir!
Tulips in tutu, ready to twirl,
Capers and hops, giving joy a whirl.

The daisies chime in with a squeaky voice,
'Looks like these petals made a choice!'
Chasing the bees in a colorful race,
In this symphony, all find their place.

A bubbling brook strums along the way,
As laughter ripples, bright as the day.
In nature's concert, we all partake,
In a vibrant dance, make no mistake!

Beneath the Canopy of Leaves

Under the boughs where shadows play,
The critters come out to dance and sway.
A raccoon dons a tux, quite refined,
While chipmunks giggle, mischievously twined.

The ferns whisper jokes to passing bees,
'Have you heard the one about the trees?'
The breeze blows softly, a giggling sound,
As acorns roll off the ground.

A wise old owl hoots, 'Keep it light,
There's laughter hidden in day and night.'
Mice scurry by, playing tag so spry,
Beneath leafy arches, watch them fly!

In this woodland wonder, fun's never far,
Where every critter is a shining star.
With laughter that rolls from branches above,
Together we thrive in this place we love!

Chasing Sunrays Through Verdant Shadows

In emerald fields where daisies prance,
I chased a ray with a silly dance.
A butterfly laughed, then took flight,
As I stumbled on grass, what a sight!

The sunbeams play on my gleeful chase,
While ants march by in their perfect race.
I tried to join, oh what a blunder,
Fell headfirst in flowers, isn't life a wonder?

With petals as pillows, I take a rest,
All creatures gather, I feel quite blessed.
A snail winks at me, I laugh out loud,
In this silly world, I'm quite proud!

As shadows stretch long in the late afternoon,
I twirl with the flowers, under a big balloon.
The sun waves goodbye, but I won't forget,
Chasing rays here, is my best bet!

Dancing Sunbeams Amidst the Green

Across the lawn, the sunbeams glide,
I join their dance with goofy pride.
A squirrel stops, gives me a stare,
As I spin around in the warm, bright air.

In laughter rings the bumblebee,
With all my twirls, he buzzes with glee.
I tripped on a root; oh dear me,
But the daisies chuckled, so wild and free.

My feet are muddy, my shirt's a mess,
But every misstep brings joy, I guess.
The clouds above are fluffing in fun,
As I dance with shadows, glowing like the sun.

When the breeze whispers sweet in my ear,
I twirl once more without any fear.
The grass beneath laughs at my silly show,
With dancing sunbeams, there's always a glow!

Texture of Life in a Floral Ballet

In hues of pink and shades of gold,
I step on petals, feeling bold.
A bumblebee dons a tiny hat,
Smirking at me like, 'Imagine that!'

The roses sigh and give a share,
Of fragrant whispers, light as air.
I try to waltz with the tulip crew,
But they just giggle, 'We can't dance like you!'

In this floral realm, with laughter rife,
Even the weeds are part of life.
I pull a daisy, it shouts, 'Oh no!'
We twirl together, putting on a show.

With dahlias nodding in playful sway,
I frolic free like a child at play.
The breeze is music, the petals are bright,
In this balletic bloom, everything feels right!

sculpting Dreams from Nature's Hands

With leaves like hands, nature sculpts away,
Crafting giggles in the light of day.
I found a twig and called it my wand,
With a splash of mud, all worries are gone.

The trees wear crowns of green and gold,
They sway with laughter, brimming with bold.
I join in their mirth, a jesting game,
Under the branches, it's never the same.

A chipmunk winks, rocks a slick little tie,
While I sculpt a dream in a ladybug's eye.
With petals for paint and sunshine for glue,
I make silly wishes; oh, if only they knew!

At dusk, as shadows stretch long and wide,
I twirl with the night, it's a whimsical ride.
Nature's a jester, a playful spree,
In this sculpted world, I'm simply me!

Secret Paths of the Green Haven

In the leafy maze, a squirrel leaps,
Wearing its acorn crown, it giggle-squeaks.
The worms hold parties, all wiggly and bright,
While the daisies dance beneath the moonlight.

Bumblebees buzz, planning their spree,
But trip on flowers, oh, woe is me!
The sunflowers watch with their tall heads turned,
As the carrots plot how their roots can be spurned.

A rabbit jokes, with a hop and a skip,
"I've got the best lettuce, care for a trip?"
The carrots reply with a leafy cheer,
"Just watch your step, you may lose a rear!"

So in this realm of green, joy will sprout,
With giggles and chuckles, there's never a doubt.
From burrows to blooms, a whimsical show,
In paths of the green haven, laughter will grow.

The Language of Blossoms

The tulips gossip in hues quite absurd,
Trading sweet secrets, not one single word.
The roses roll eyes, with petals in flair,
"Did you see that bee? It landed—oh, where?"

Petunias chuckle, their colors so bright,
As daisies declare they'll dance through the night.
"Watch out for the wind!" yells the poppy with glee,
"It steals all our hats; we must hide with esprit!"

The violets snipe with a flick of their stems,
"Those pansies think they're quite cute with their hems!"
But lilies just nod, their grandeur speaks loud,
While cacti wear prickers, they're humble but proud.

So here in this chatter, with grace and with jest,
The flowers unite, with humor expressed.
In a world where petals and laughter entwine,
The language of blossoms is simply divine.

Soft Glances on Dew-Kissed Leaves

Morning breaks gently with laughter and cheer,
As droplets of dew get up for the year.
Each leaf wears the sparkle like jewels of glee,
As the bugs start to dance, oh, what a spree!

The ladybugs laugh as they twirl in the sun,
"Let's show off our spots; we're the cutest—bar none!"
While beetles debate if they're smooth or they're rough,
"Oh come on, dear friends, we're all equally tough!"

A caterpillar sighs, feeling down in the muck,
Where's the bright butterfly, the luck or just luck?
But from leaf to leaf floats a fluttering tease,
"In time you'll be splendid, just wait, if you please!"

So soft are the glances on leaves in the morn,
With nature's own humor, sweet smiles are reborn.
In tiny green worlds, the fun will arise,
While the dew-kissed leaves twinkle like little wise eyes.

Starlight on Morning Blooms

When stars take a bow, the flowers can't sleep,
Whispering secrets, they giggle and peep.
The night watchman owl, with a wink of his eye,
Just hoots a soft chorus, "Oh, give it a try!"

The moon grins down, fully adorned with gold,
"Dance, little blooms, let your stories unfold!"
While the petals keep winking as if to outshine,
"We'll steal all the dreams—just wait for the sign!"

A bumblebee buzzes past, feeling quite spry,
"Did you hear that last joke? Oh my, oh my!"
As crickets provide the night's joyful score,
The daisies join in; it's never a bore.

With each gentle rustle, the laughter takes flight,
A tapestry woven from whispers of light.
In starlit embraces, let joy brightly bloom,
For every flower knows how to lighten the gloom.

Jasmine Dreams on Moonlit Nights

In the moon's soft glow, cats prance with delight,
Chasing shadows that dance, oh what a sight!
Beneath jasmine blooms, they twirl and they spin,
Caught in a dream where the laughter begins.

Fireflies flicker, a disco in air,
While frogs in their tuxedos croak tunes without care.
The crickets all join in a whimsical band,
As the raccoons snap selfies, oh isn't that grand?

With petals like pillows, they nestle and play,
Sipping sweet nectar, a party ballet.
Ngger skies twinkle, like glittering charms,
While the night holds tight in its twinkling arms.

So here in this night, with laughter so bright,
The creatures unite in a whimsical flight.
Waving goodbye to the moon's gentle tease,
With dreams that are funny, just like the breeze.

Nature's Symphony in Colorful Harmony

In the garden of giggles, where daisies peep through,
Bumblebees bouncing, wearing small rubber shoes.
Chirping and chortling, the finches compose,
A tune filled with laughter, as everyone knows.

Ladybugs tap dance on leaves with a beat,
While tulips in capes prepare for the feat.
The sunflowers twirl to a jazzy parade,
As dandelions puff like confetti displayed.

The squirrels are jesters in this vibrant play,
Hiding acorns, then laughing, 'Oh not today!'
The backdrop's a canvas of yellow and green,
Where nature's own laughter brightens the scene.

As butterflies flutter, making wishes take flight,
Every tailwind of joy feels just so right.
In this symphony lush, where fun meets the eye,
Nature itself is a stand-up, oh my!

Light and Shadow on Leafy Visions

In the leafy domain where shadows do prance,
Wombats wear sunglasses and happily dance.
The sunlight swings low, a playful slide,
As the babbling brook giggles and glides.

Parrots paint jokes on the canvas of trees,
Telling tales of the winds and the oft-happy bees.
With shadows as partners in their silly game,
Every leaf whispers secrets, none of them tame.

The tadpoles plot mischief; oh what a scheme!
While the fish roll their eyes, like, 'What a dream!'
Jumping in puddles, the frogs start to sing,
And the dragonflies buzz about every fling.

So in this bright corner, with laughter all around,
Light plays its tricks while the shadows astound.
It's a party of nature, with jokes that won't end,
In the leafy delight where giggles transcend.

The Enchanted Echoes of Spring

In the light of dawn's embrace,
The frogs croak in a silly race.
Bees wear tiny little hats,
And dance with joy among the mats.

Daisies gossip with the bees,
While petals tickle at the knees.
A squirrel juggles acorns high,
As butterflies just swoosh on by.

Worms play chess beneath the dirt,
While ladybugs just flaunt their skirt.
It's a circus filled with glee,
In this realm of jolly spree.

Frogs and flowers form a band,
Playing tunes that are quite grand.
With laughter echoing so clear,
The springtime fun is always here.

Flowered Memories of a Forgotten Day

Amidst the blooms, a tale is spun,
Of past escapes and silly fun.
A dandelion dressed in gold,
Recounts the mischief from days of old.

Tulips gossip in a ballet,
While a snail tries to join the fray.
A bumblebee, quite out of breath,
Claims he won the race, but met his death!

Picking petals, hearts did yearn,
As daisies taught us all to learn.
From every giggle shared with pride,
A hint of joy we cannot hide.

The roses laugh in fragrant tones,
As butterflies fly near the stones.
In these memories wrapped in cheer,
A sunny smile will always be near.

A Kaleidoscope of Living Colors

A rainbow bursts from every bloom,
While clovers plot to gain some room.
Their whispers float on warming airs,
Deciding who has the best flares.

Petunias prance with vibrant flair,
While sunflowers boast their solar hair.
A playful breeze begins to twirl,
Making petals dance and whirl.

The violets hide, they wear a frown,
As pansies try to steal their crown.
A sunflower team performs a stunt,
As tulips cheer with every punt.

In this tapestry of wild hues,
Even weeds share their silly views.
With laughter painting every shade,
The colors burst as pranks are played.

The Petal's Embrace at Dusk

At dusk, the petals yawn and sigh,
As butterflies prepare to fly.
Unfurling dreams of evening light,
They giggle softly, a playful sight.

A daisy whispers to a rose,
"Wanna share a sunset pose?"
They strike a pose, all tongue and fun,
While crickets play as day is done.

The last bee flits with flair so bold,
Hoping to find a story told.
He lands, but slips—oh what a mess!
The flowers chuckle, they can't suppress!

As shadows merge and stars appear,
The blossoms whisper tales sincere.
Yet laughter lingers, ever bright,
In the fading hues of warm twilight.

The Stillness of Blooming Thoughts

In a patch of green where daisies dance,
A squirrel squeaks his cheeky chance.
Bees argue over who gets the pie,
While ants just march, they won't comply.

Butterflies flaunt their vibrant wings,
Confusing folks with all their flings.
A gnome in the corner shakes his head,
Thinking of mischief while folks are fed.

The tulips gossip in colors bright,
About the sun that stole the night.
A hedgehog snores, all cozy in weeds,
While a robin plots for tasty seeds.

So laughter bubbles in hidden nooks,
Amidst the whims of nature'sooks.
Each bloom a story, each leaf a joke,
In this wild realm where fun's bespoke.

Imagined Landscapes in Blooming Silence

Under a bough with acorns spilling,
A snail slid by, rather thrilling.
He wore a hat, or was it a shell?
Imagining kingdoms, he brewed quite well.

A little frog crooned his love tune,
To a cabbage that smiled like the moon.
His croak a melody, a grand charade,
While carrots giggled in their green parade.

Chasing shadows with chuckles soft,
Buttercups swayed like a dance oft.
A hedgehog twirled, lost in his dreams,
While radishes plotted in curious schemes.

With every tickle of the breeze,
Laughter flows through the leafy trees.
Invented tales from flora so bright,
Where silence hides all giggles in flight.

Refreshing Raindrops and Venus' Moons

Raindrops tap, a funny ballet,
Dancing on rooftops in wild array.
A puddle reflects the clouds' own grin,
As lipstick blooms on a bumble bee's chin.

Venus winks, she sees the show,
While mushrooms laugh in their covert glow.
A worm in the mud sings fine and clear,
As flowers sip water, downing their beer.

With each splash, a joy is born,
In this chaotic, cheerful morn.
A snail in a slick race, oh what fun!
He slows for a sip, then races the sun.

So let the raindrops drop where they may,
In this playful scene, we'll dance and sway.
Each splash a chuckle, each droplet a cheer,
In the fun of the moment, we hold dear.

Whirling Leaves Amidst the Autumn Glow

Leaves twirl round with a giggly spin,
Spying on pumpkins wearing a grin.
A squirrel collects acorns, pretty sly,
While a crow caws loud from way up high.

Crisp air tickles as laughter floats,
Through rustling woods where nature gloats.
A fox in a scarf just can't sit still,
Chasing his tail down the hill with a thrill.

Chattering chums in colors so bright,
Band together to scare off the night.
With every swish of the breeze anew,
Trees chuckle softly, their laughter askew.

Every crunch of leaves beneath our feet,
Echoes a joke that feels oh-so sweet.
In the fading sunlight's amber glow,
Together we dance in the fall's silly show.

www.ingramcontent.com/pod-product-compliance
Lightning Source LLC
Chambersburg PA
CBHW051629160426
43209CB00004B/574